Arthur Cleveland Coxe

Mozarabic Collects

Translated and arranged from the ancient liturgy of the Spanish church

Arthur Cleveland Coxe

Mozarabic Collects
Translated and arranged from the ancient liturgy of the Spanish church

ISBN/EAN: 9783744796637

Printed in Europe, USA, Canada, Australia, Japan

Cover: Foto ©Lupo / pixelio.de

More available books at **www.hansebooks.com**

Mozarabic Collects

TRANSLATED AND ARRANGED

FROM THE

ANCIENT LITURGY OF THE SPANISH CHURCH

BY THE

REV. CHAS. R. HALE, S. T. D.

✦

WITH A PREFACE BY

THE RT. REV. A. CLEVELAND COXE, D. D.

Bishop of Western New York.

NEW YORK
JAMES POTT, Publisher
12 Astor Place
1881.

IN REVERENT AND LOVING

MEMORY OF

WILLIAM ROLLINSON WHITTINGHAM,

BISHOP OF MARYLAND,

1840-1879.

———

"FORTY YEARS LONG"

A LEADER OF GOD'S ISRAEL,

HE HAS PASSED OVER INTO THE LAND OF REST.

———

'GIVE US GRACE, O LORD, SO TO FOLLOW HIS GOOD EXAM-
PLE, THAT WITH HIM WE MAY BE PARTAKERS OF THY HEAV-
ENLY KINGDOM.'

PREFACE.

WHAT little is known in our communion of the Mozarabic Rite, so called, is generally derived from the genuine erudition of Neale, from what Palmer less accurately tells us, and from an inspection of the material preserved in Migne's *Patrologia*. It is surprising how little has been wrought out from this field, and with how little success the learned have tried to account for the name itself. To call it "The Gothic Rite," as many do, is very misleading. It is, in its essential and original parts, the ancient Spanish Liturgy, as Neale has lucidly shewn; and it is interesting more especially for two reasons: (1) it is akin to the ancient Gallican Rite, and (2) it so far partakes of an Ephesine spirit, as to be justly styled a link between the usages of East and West.

From the time, when, in God's Providence, I was called to a place on "the Mexican Commission," it has been my ardent hope and desire to see the attention of the reformed Mexican Church, turned to these ancient sources of her own historic faith; and to induce her divines to use them, precisely as our reformers used the old Anglican Offices, in renewing the Primitive Worship and its simple but sublime ceremonial. Whatever concessions have been made *pro tempore* to present exigencies and difficulties, I am justified by the Reports, now published, in saying that the Commission itself has, over and over again, recognized the principle thus expressed, and cherishes the hope that it will yet be accepted by the Mexican "Old Catholics" as their true policy, on every account; but, also, as due to the terms of their "Covenant" with our Catholic and Apostolic Church. We have no right to impose on them our convictions, however; and we must wait till the Holy Spirit, whose presence and power are so evidently with them, enables them, by study and larger commerce with loving hearts among us, to "work out their own Salvation," in the practical way we suggest.

Absorbed in the pressing duties of my Episcopate, I have from the first, relied on my beloved brother Dr. Hale, whom I have known and conferred with, from the days of his pupillage, to work in this old mine *for* me and *with* me; and I am pleased with this opportunity of thanking him for his unwearied labours, in bringing forth treasures " new and old," from Spanish Antiquity: they are *old* and primitive in themselves: they are largely *new* to his brethren·

He has compiled an admirable office for the Holy

Eucharist; and a Baptismal Office, also, from such materials; and I trust they may soon see the light, with an introductory *Excursus* and with the *Notes* with which he is so capable of enriching the work. The COLLECTS herewith presented are a mere specimen of their Editor's entire work, but they are not an inconsiderable portion of it, and they may, by God's blessing, awaken attention to the subject, and thus promote his ultimate desires and purposes, with which I sympathize, ardently; not only because of my respect for him, but rather because of the importance of the subject to Catholic Reconstruction and Reform in Mexico and elsewhere.

I have before me the important work of Lorenzana, published in 1770, with the probable design of favouring the introduction of the Old Spanish Rite into Mexico. He had been one of the Canons of the Royal Foundation, in Toledo, which preserved the Ancient Spanish Liturgy (interpolated indeed by Cardinal Ximenes) and was made Archbishop of Mexico. With him, one of his fellow-canons, who had become Bishop of Los Angelos, was a fellow labourer, in the same cause. By the aid of Neale's criticisms, and the general principles of Primitive Worship so admirably expounded by the late Archdeacon Freeman, it would not be a difficult task for

our Mexican brethren, to make this work of Lorenzana a most useful instrument of influence with their
unreformed countrymen.

It is Dr. Hale's idea, and I sincerely share it with
him, that the Commission of our own Church, now
engaged in Liturgical Inquiry, might not improbably
find some material for their labours in the same direc-
tion.   Nor do I overlook the practical object he has
kept in mind, of enriching the devotional resources
of pious members of the Church, for their private
communings with God, in the fellowship of His
Saints.

But, in any case, the labours of Dr. Hale will be
most useful to some; and I trust this publication
may, by God's blessing, lead to such great results as
His blessed Spirit delights to produce, from ventures
of faith the most humble and unpretending.

A. CLEVELAND COXE,

Bishop of Western New York.

BUFFALO, FEAST OF THE
    PURIFICATION B. V. M., 1881.

CONTENTS.

The Collects

SEASONS OF THE CHRISTIAN YEAR.

Advent to Christmas.

O GOD, Who by Angelic Choirs wast pleased to announce the coming of Thy Son, our Lord Jesus Christ, and didst, by the heralding of angels, proclaim, Glory to God on High, and on earth peace, good will towards men; Grant that we may so pass our time here in Thy fear, that at Thy Son's second coming we may rejoice before Him with exceeding joy. *Amen.*

Through Thy mercy, O oúr God, Who art blessed, and dost live, and govern all things, world without end. *Amen.*

Christmas to Septuagesima.

O BLESSED Saviour, Who, as the Prophets foretold, born (as at this time)* of a pure Virgin, didst come to be a Treasure to the poor, a Light to

---

* On and after the Epiphany omit the words in parenthesis.

them that sat in darkness, the Strength of the weak,
the Health of the sick, and the Resurrection of the
dead; Grant that through Thy glorious Nativity we
may be loosed from the bonds of our sins, and may
ever rejoice in Thy praise. *Amen.*

Through Thy mercy, O our God, Who art blessed,
and dost live, and govern all things, world without
end. *Amen.*

Septuagesima to Lent.

(The same as from Trinity Sunday to Advent. See below.)

Lent.

LET all the world hear Thee, O Lord, the rich and
the poor bow down their hearts unto Thee; Thee
only may our souls seek after, Thee may we praise,
with all Thy Saints, in eternal joy, and find Thee
our exceeding great Reward. *Amen.*

Through Thy mercy, O our God, Who art blessed,
and dost live, and govern all things, world without
end. *Amen.*

Easter to Ascension.

TO Thee we ascribe glory, O Christ our God, and
we pray Thee that as Thou didst vouchsafe to
die for our sins, and didst, on the third day, rise from

the dead in glory, so, freed from sin through Thee, we may find in Thee perpetual joy. *Amen.*

Through Thy mercy, O our God, Who art blessed, and dost live, and govern all things, world without end. *Amen.*

Ascension to Whitsun-day.

O LORD, our Saviour, Who didst ascend up on High in glory, in the sight of Thy disciples; Grant that in Thee our hearts and minds may so be lifted up above the things of earth, that we may not be ashamed before Thee when Thou comest to be our Judge. *Amen.*

Through Thy mercy, O our God, Who art blessed, and dost live, and govern all things, world without end. *Amen.*

Whitsun-day to Trinity Sunday.

O GOD the Holy Ghost, Who, with the Father and the Son together, art worshipped and glorified; Teach us to know the truth, and make us ever to rejoice in the truth. *Amen.*

Through Thy mercy, O our God, Who art blessed, and dost live, and govern all things, world without end. *Amen.*

Trinity Sunday to Advent.

TO Thee, O Lord, all power belongeth in the Highest, to Thee the Church on earth sings Glory; Grant, we humbly pray Thee, Almighty God, that like as we show forth Thy praise, so Thou wouldest ever hearken unto the voice of our prayers. *Amen.*

Through Thy mercy, O our God, Who art blessed, and dost live, and govern all things, world without end. *Amen.*

Saints' Days.

O GOD, Who didst give unto Thy blessed Saints grace, through faith, to despise the world and to follow after Thee; Mercifully hear our prayers, and grant that all care for what is evil may die in us, and that our hearts may ever glow with love to Thee. *Amen.*

Through Thy mercy, O our God, Who art blessed, and dost live, and govern all things, world without end. *Amen.*

The Collects

FOR THE

SUNDAYS AND OTHER HOLY DAYS

THROUGHOUT THE YEAR.

The First Sunday in Advent.

O LORD Jesus Christ, Who at the first coming of Thy glory didst humble Thyself because of our sins; Grant that at Thy second coming, our sins done away by Thy mercy, we may be numbered with Thy Saints in glory everlasting; Through Thy merits, O Blessed Saviour, Who, with the Father and the Holy Ghost, livest and reignest, ever one God, world without end. *Amen.*

The Second Sunday in Advent.

O GOD, Who, by the mouth of Thy holy prophets, didst promise that Thine Only-begotten Son should come in the flesh for us, and be born of a pure virgin, and hast in these last days fulfilled Thy word; Grant, we beseech Thee, that when He Who came once to redeem the world cometh to be our Judge, we may not be ashamed before Him at His coming; Through the merits of the same, Thy Son, Jesus Christ our Lord. *Amen.*

The Third Sunday in Advent.

O GOD, our Heavenly Father, Who didst send Thy messengers to tell of the birth of Thy Son, that men might believe on Him; Grant that, hearing Thee, we may repent of our sins, and seek our heavenly inheritance, so that we, who profess Christ, may not for our works be condemned before the glory of Thy majesty; Grant this, we humbly beseech Thee, for the sake of the same, Thy Son, Jesus Christ our Lord. *Amen.*

The Fourth Sunday in Advent.

O LORD, raise up we pray Thee Thy power, and come to deliver us, that we, who are oppressed by temptations, may be so defended by Thy might, that the hosts of the enemy may never prevail against us; Hear us of Thy mercy, O Lord Christ, Who, with the Father and the Holy Ghost, livest and reignest, ever one God, world without end. *Amen.*

The Nativity of our LORD,

Commonly called Christmas Day.

O LORD Jesus Christ, Who, Very God of Very God, didst deign for us to become a little child, that the world which Thou didst make might through Thee be saved; Grant that, as unto us a Child is born, unto us a Son is given, we, born again through Thee, may ever remain in the number of God's faithful children; Through Thy merits, O Blessed Saviour, Who, with the Father and the Holy Ghost, livest and reignest, ever one God, world without end. *Amen.*

The Sunday after Christmas.

O GOD, the Son of God, whose name endureth forever, and Who yet didst take upon Thee our nature to redeem the world; Grant that we, who are glad at Thy first coming, may rejoice in Thy full salvation when Thou comest to be our Judge; Through Thy mercy, O our God, Who art blessed, and dost live, and govern all things, world without end. *Amen.*

The Circumcision of Christ.

O JESUS, our Saviour and our Lord, Who, by the proclamation of Thy grace, didst take from our necks the yoke of the law, and remove the burden from our shoulders to Thine own; Grant to the prayers of Thy Church, that it may joyfully serve Thee here, and behold Thy blissful presence with fullness of joy hereafter; Through Thy mercy, O our God, Who art blessed, and dost live, and govern all things, world without end. *Amen.*

And this :

O GOD, Whose days are without beginning and without end; Grant us, we humbly pray thee, throughout this year, whose beginning we dedicate to Thee, such prosperity as Thou seest to be good for us, and make us to abound in such works as may be pleasing unto Thee; Through Jesus Christ our Lord. *Amen.*

The former of these two Collects, shall serve for every day after, unto the Epiphany.

The Epiphany,
Or Manifestation of Christ to the Gentiles.

O JESUS Christ our King, Whose sign to the Wise Men was a bright shining star; Enlighten us ever by Thy grace, and fill us with all wisdom and spiritual understanding; Grant this of Thy goodness, O our Lord, Whose kingdom and dominion endure throughout all ages. *Amen.*

This Collect shall serve until the Saturday evening following.

The First Sunday after the Epiphany.

O LORD God, who dost ever hear the voice of them that cry unto Thee, and shewest tender mercy unto them that are distressed; Grant that we, hating the vanity of this world, and renouncing its deceits, may find in Christ our eternal and exceeding great Reward; Grant this, we beseech Thee, for the sake of the same, Thy Blessed Son, our Saviour. *Amen.*

The Second Sunday after the Epiphany.

O ALMIGHTY God, Who didst raise up Thy Blessed Son in righteousness, making Him manifest in the flesh; Grant that we may ever follow Him both in word and deed, so that, hearing Him with the hearing of the heart, we may be partakers of His glory; Through the same, Thy Son, Jesus Christ our Lord. *Amen.*

The Third Sunday after the Epiphany.

O GOD the Father Almighty; Incline Thine ear unto our prayers, and grant us the fullness of charity and peace; that we, whose faith is in Thy mercy, may ever live in hope and charity; Through Jesus Christ our Lord. *Amen.*

The Fourth Sunday after the Epiphany.

GRANT unto us, O Lord our Strength, to have a true love of Thy Holy Name, so that, trusting in Thy grace, we may fear no earthly evil, and set our hearts upon no earthly good, but may rejoice at last in Thy full salvation; Through Jesus Christ our Lord. *Amen.*

The Fifth Sunday after the Epiphany.

O ONLY-BEGOTTEN Son of God the Father, Who, to save the world, didst deign to take upon Thee our nature, and so humbling Thyself didst open up again to fallen man the way to Paradise; Do away, we pray Thee, our iniquities, so that, cleansed from our sins, we may be inheritors with Thy Saints of Thy heavenly kingdom; Through Thy mercy, O our God, Who art blessed, and dost live, and govern all things, world without end. *Amen.*

The Sixth Sunday after the Epiphany.

O GOD, the Author of peace; Grant, we beseech Thee, that Thy faithful people may be so held in the bonds of charity, that the peaceful may remain in peace, and that those who differ may be reconciled by Thy mercy; Through Jesus Christ, Thy Son, our Lord. *Amen.*

The Third Sunday before Lent,
Commonly called Septuagesima Sunday.

O GOD, good and gracious, and of great mercy unto all that call upon Thee; Let our cry, we beseech Thee, enter into Thine ears, and of Thy tender mercy do away our offences, that we, who are bowed down with our sins, may serve Thee faithfully here, and stand in Thy presence in glory hereafter; Through Jesus Christ our Lord. *Amen.*

The Second Sunday before Lent,
Commonly called Sexagesima Sunday.

O GOD, Who so lovedst the world that Thou didst give Thine Only-Begotten Son to reconcile the earthly with the heavenly; Grant that, loving Thee above all things, we may love our friends in Thee, and our enemies for Thee; Through the same, Thy Son, Jesus Christ our Lord. *Amen.*

The Sunday next before Lent,
Commonly called Quinquagesima Sunday.

O GOD of all mercies, O Lord of all might; Bestow upon us, we pray Thee, the abundance of Thy goodness, remove our feet from evil, and enable us to walk in the path which leads to Thee; Through Jesus Christ, Thy Son our Lord. *Amen.*

The First Day of Lent,
Commonly called Ash-Wednesday.

O GOD, Who desirest not the death of a sinner, but rather that he should turn and live; Look with pity upon the weakness of our mortal nature, and grant that we, who confess that we are but ashes, and that for our wickedness we most justly return to the dust, may obtain of Thee the forgiveness of all our sins, and the blessings promised to the penitent; Through Jesus Christ our Lord. *Amen.*

And this:

A LMIGHTY and everlasting God, Who hast mercy upon all men, and hatest nothing that Thou hast made, and dost forgive the sins of all them that are penitent; Grant, for the glory of Thy Name, that we, who humble ourselves as in dust and ashes before Thee, may obtain of Thee perfect remission and forgiveness; Through Jesus Christ our Lord. *Amen.*

The former of these two collects is for Ash-Wednesday only; the latter shall serve until the Sunday following.

The First Sunday in Lent.

O CHRIST, the Son of God, Who, for our sakes, didst fast forty days, and didst suffer Thyself to be tempted; Grant that we may not be led astray through any temptations; and, since man doth not live by bread alone, nourish our souls with heavenly food; Through Thy mercy, O our God, Who art blessed, and dost live, and govern all things, world without end. *Amen.*

The Second Sunday in Lent.

O JESUS, Son of God the Father, the Fount ot Life everlasting; Give unto us who thirst, living water, give unto us eternal life; Hear us of Thy mercy, O Christ Jesus, Whom, with the Father and the Holy Ghost, we worship and glorify, ever one God, world without end. *Amen.*

The Third Sunday in Lent.

O LORD Jesus Christ, Who, by Thine almighty power, didst open the eyes of the blind, and reveal Thyself unto them; Turn away, we pray Thee, our eyes from vanity, and make us truly to love Thee; Through Thy mercy, O our God, Who art blessed, and dost live, and govern all things, world without end. *Amen.*

The Fourth Sunday in Lent.

O LORD, our Light and our Salvation; Remove from us the darkness of sorrow and of igno-rance, enlighten us with true wisdom, and give us ever a sure hope in Thee, Whom, with the Father and the Holy Ghost, we worship and glorify, ever one God, world without end. *Amen.*

The Fifth Suuday in Lent.

O HOLY Jesus, most loving Saviour, Who madest Lazarus to hear Thy voice, and come forth from the sepulchre; Grant that we, hearing Thee with the hearing of the heart, may arise from our sins, and serve Thee in newness of life; through Thy mercy, O our God, Who art blessed, and dost live, and govern all things, world without end. *Amen.*

Palm Sunday.

O LORD Jesus Christ, before Whom, entering into Jerusalem, great multitudes waved palm branches, and cried Hosanna; We humbly beseech Thy Divine Majesty to save us now from our sins, and make us to rejoice in Thee, Who didst come to redeem us; Through Thy mercy, O our God, Who art blessed, and dost live, and govern all things, world without end. *Amen.*

And this :

O GOD, the Son of God, Who didst deign to take upon Thee our nature, and to suffer death upon the cross for us; By the mystery of Thy Passion set us free, we pray Thee, from death eternal; Through Thy mercy, O our God, Who art blessed, and dost live, and govern all things, world without end. *Amen.*

The former of these Collects is for Palm Sunday only, the latter shall serve until Good Friday.

Good Friday.

O GOD, the Son of God, who didst suffer for us, the just for the unjust; Save us by the shame of Thy Passion, and clothe us with the robe of Thy righteousness, so that, through the unmerited suffering of Thy death, we may escape the punishment our sins have deserved. *Amen.*

And this:

H EAR the sorrowful sighing of Thy Church, O Lord, Who for her didst suffer death upon the cross, let her, whose sole trust is in what Thou didst endure for her, never ᴄ: be put to shame, be her support in all trials, and crown her at last with glory everlasting. *Amen.*

Easter Even.

O LORD Jesus Christ, Who didst, for our sins, endure the cross and the grave, and then didst, on the third day, rise again from the tomb; Grant that by Thy Blood we may be cleansed from sin, and that, as we are buried with Thee in Baptism, so by Thy grace, we may share in the first Resurrection; Through Thy mercy, O our God, Who art blessed, and dost live, and govern all things, world without end. *Amen.*

Easter Day.

O LORD Jesus Christ, Who didst die for the sins of the whole world, and, as at this time, didst rise from the dead; By Thy Resurrection mortify and kill all vices in us; and as, by Thy Cross and Passion, Thou didst destroy the power of death, make us to share in the blessed life; Through Thy merits, O Blessed Saviour, Who dost live, and govern all things, world without end. *Amen.*

This collect shall serve also for Easter Monday and Tuesday.

The First Sunday after Easter.

O LION of the Tribe of Judah, O Root of David; Enlighten our hearts and minds with Thy true wisdom, that we, who now rejoice in Thy Resurrection, may, in Thy Kingdom, join with Thy Blessed Ones, and with all the Heavenly Host, in praising Thy Glorious Name, Who, with the Father, and the Holy Ghost, livest and reignest, ever one God, world without end. *Amen.*

The Second Sunday after Easter.

O GOD, our Light and our Salvation; Grant that by Thy holy inspiration we may know what we ought to do, and that by Thy grace we may be enabled to perform the same; Through Jesus Christ our Lord. *Amen.*

The Third Sunday after Easter.

O CHRIST, The Son of God, the Lamb that was slain, but is now risen in glory; Hearken, we beseech Thee, to our prayers, and grant that we may die to all that is evil, and rise to good works; Through Thy mercy, O our God, Who art blessed, and dost live, and govern all things, world without end. *Amen.*

The Fourth Sunday after Easter.

O LORD Jesus Christ, very God and very Man, Who changest not, but art holy in all Thy works; Take away from us, we humbly beseech Thee, all unbelief, and fill us with the gifts of Thy grace; Through Thy mercy, O our God, Who art blessed, and dost live, and govern all things, world without end. *Amen.*

The Fifth Sunday after Easter.

O LORD, save us, we pray Thee, who hope in Thee, comfort us, according to Thy word, whom Thou hast redeemed with Thy most Precious Blood, and grant us, with Thee, perpetual joy and felicity, where sighing is at an end, and sorrow cannot come; Through Thy mercy, O our God, Who art blessed, and dost live, and govern all things, world without end. *Amen.*

The Rogation Days.

O LORD, our God, Who art plenteous in goodness to all those who confess their sins unto Thee; Have mercy upon us, Thine unworthy servants, grant us, we pray Thee, fruitful seasons, that our land may yield her increase; and make the good seed of Thy word sink deep into our hearts, and bring forth fruit in our lives, to the glory of Thy Name; Through Jesus Christ our Lord. *Amen.*

The Ascension Day.

O LORD, the King of Glory, Who, when Thou hadst fulfilled all that the Prophets had spoken of Thee, didst, through the Eternal Doors, ascend to Thy Father's Throne, and open the Kingdom of

Heaven to all believers; Grant that whilst Thou dost reign in Heaven, we may not be bowed down to the things of earth, but that our hearts may there be lifted up whither our redemption is gone before; Through Thy mercy, O our God, Who, with the Father and the Holy Ghost, livest and reignest, ever one God, world without end. *Amen.*

This collect shall serve until the Saturday evening following.

The Sunday after Ascension Day.

O LORD, strong and mighty, the Lord of Hosts, the King of Glory; cleanse our hearts from sin, keep our hands pure, and turn away our minds from vanity, so that, at the last, we may stand in Thy Holy Place, and receive blessing from Thee, Whom, with the Father and the Holy Ghost, we worship and glorify, as one God, world without end. *Amen.*

Whitsun-day.

O HOLY Ghost, Who, as at this time, didst descend upon the Apostles in the likeness of fiery tongues; Take away all vices from our hearts, and fill us with all wisdom and spiritual understanding; Grant this, O Blessed Spirit, Who, with the Father and the Son, livest and reignest, ever one God, world without end. *Amen.*

This collect shall serve also for Monday and Tuesday in Whit-sun-week.

Trinity Sunday.

O FATHER, Son and Holy Ghost, Three Persons, but One God; Enlighten, we pray Thee, our hearts and minds, that we, steadfast in the true faith, and ever shining in good works, may attain at last to the life everlasting; Through Thy mercy, O our God, Who art blessed, and dost live, and govern all things, world without end. *Amen.*

The First Sunday after Trinity.

O GOD, Who hast granted peace to the angels by a perpetual decree, and hast made a way for men also to share in it, grant unto us, Thy servants, that we may pass our time here in the desire of peace, and may have our portion forever in the Kingdom of Peace; through Thy Son, Jesus Christ, our Lord. *Amen.*

The Second Sunday after Trinity.

O GOD, Who only art holy, and Who dost by Thy grace purify the unholy: Cleanse us, we humbly beseech Thee, from every spot of sin, so that, justified by Thee, our names may be written in Heaven; Grant this, for the sake of Jesus Christ, our most Blessed Lord and Saviour. *Amen.*

The Third Sunday after Trinity.

O LORD, our God, Who hast commanded us to speak righteousness, and to judge uprightly; Grant that iniquity may not be found in our mouths, nor wickedness in our minds, but that, from pure hearts, we may speak those things that are right; Through Jesus Christ our Lord. *Amen.*

The Fourth Sunday after Trinity.

O CHRIST, our Lord and our Eternal Redeemer; Grant unto us such fellowship in Thy sufferings, that, filled with Thine Holy Spirit, we may subdue the flesh to the spirit, and the spirit to Thee, and at last attain to the glory of Thy resurrection; Through Thy mercy, O our God, Who art blessed, and dost live, and govern all things, world without end. *Amen.*

The Fifth Sunday after Trinity.

O GOD, the Father Almighty, Grant us to have in Thee the light of knowledge, and the fulness of all virtue, that, while we seek for the gifts of learn-

ing, we may never depart from Thee, Who art the
Fountain of all wisdom ; Through Jesus Christ, Thy
Son, our Lord. *Amen.*

The Sixth Sunday after Trinity.

O CHRIST, the Power of God and the Wisdom
of God; Defend us, we pray Thee, by Thy
grace, that we may never stand in the way of sinners,
but by Thine aid may ever run, with a free heart, in
the way of thy commandments ; Through Thy mercy,
O our God, Who art blessed, and dost live, and govern all things, world without end. *Amen.*

The Seventh Sunday after Trinity.

O LORD Jesus Christ, the Rest of the Angels and
of all the Saints; Grant unto Thy People to
find in Thee deliverance from all sin, and rest from
every burden, so that, joining with Angels and Arch-
angels in blessing Thee, they may in all and through
all things be blessed by Thee ; Through Thy mercy, O
our God, Who art blessed, and dost live, and govern
all things, world without end. *Amen.*

The Eighth Sunday after Trinity.

O GOD, Whose Only-Begotten Son did hang
upon the Cross for us, and there pay with His
blood the price of our Redemption, that we, through

His death, might receive the adoption of sons; Give us grace, although unworthy, with true faith to call Thee Father; Through the same, Thy Son, Jesus Christ our Lord. *Amen.*

The Ninth Sunday after Trinity.

B E Thou, O Lord, our Refuge, and govern us as Thou didst our fathers, that like as Thou didst show unto them Thy goodness, so we too may share in Thy blessings; Through Jesus Christ, Thy Son, our Lord. *Amen.*

The Tenth Sunday after Trinity.

O LORD God, the Father Almighty, Inspirer of Prayer, and its ready Hearer, Lend, we pray Thee, a merciful ear unto our cry, and of Thy great pity loose the bonds of our sins; Through Jesus Christ, Thy Son, our Lord. *Amen.*

The Eleventh Sunday after Trinity.

O MERCIFUL God, Who didst justify the publican, who, standing afar off, and beating his breast, confessed his sin unto Thee; Grant unto us Thy servants, meekly acknowledging our unworthiness, and supplicating Thy favor, the forgiveness of all our sins; Through Thy mercy, and for the sake of Jesus Christ, Thy Son, our Saviour. *Amen.*

The Twelfth Sunday after Trinity.

O GOD, with Whom is the Well of Life, and in Whose Light we shall see light; Give unto us, when we thirst, living water, and enlighten our darkened minds with heavenly light; Through Jesus Christ our Lord. *Amen.*

The Thirteenth Sunday after Trinity.

O LORD Almighty, the only Begotten Son of the Father; Loose us from the bonds of our sins, and fill us with all spiritual gifts, that so, Thy grace preventing and following us, we may be Thy faithful servants here, and be numbered with Thy saints in glory hereafter; Through Thy mercy, O our God, Who art blessed, and dost live, and govern all things, world without end. *Amen.*

The Fourteenth Sunday after Trinity.

O ALMIGHTY God, our Heavenly Father; Renew in us, we humbly pray Thee, the gifts of Thy mercy, increase our faith, strengthen our hope, enlighten our understanding, enlarge our charity, and make us ever ready to serve Thee, both in body and soul; Through Jesus Christ, Thy Son, our Lord. *Amen.*

The Fifteenth Sunday after Trinity.

REMEMBER, O Lord, we pray Thee, that we are but dust, and behold the contrition of our hearts, and grant that we, who through the weakness of the flesh cannot but fall, may by Thy mighty power be lifted up; Through Jesus Christ, Thy Son, our Lord. *Amen.*

The Sixteenth Sunday after Trinity.

O ALMIGHTY God, Who art the author of everlasting felicity; Sustain and comfort us, we pray Thee, in all the trials of this present life, and grant unto us at last, in Thy presence, fulness of joy, and pleasure for evermore; Through Jesus Christ our Lord. *Amen.*

The Seventeenth Sunday after Trinity.

O LORD, Who lovest unanimity, and dwellest in a peaceful heart; Grant, we beseech Thee, to all Thy faithful people, true peace and mutual charity; Through Jesus Christ our Lord. *Amen.*

The Eighteenth Sunday after Trinity.

O CHRIST, the Alpha and the Omega, the Beginning and the Ending, the Root and the Offspring of David; Mercifully grant unto us, our King and our Saviour, that we may serve Thee faithfully here, and continue Thine forever; Through Thy merits, O our God, Who art blessed, and dost live, and govern all things, world without end. *Amen.*

The Nineteenth Sunday after Trinity.

O LORD Jesus Christ, Who art the Light of the blind, the Way of the erring, and the Resurrection of the dead; Enlighten the darkness of our hearts and minds, bring sinners to repentance, and make us to live in Thee and for Thee, Whom, with the Father and the Holy Ghost, we worship and glorify, ever one God, world without end. *Amen.*

The Twentieth Sunday after Trinity.

O LORD Jesus Christ, make us to live soberly, righteously, and godly, in this present world, looking for the blessed hope and Thy glorious appearing, so that, running in the way of Thy commandments, we may attain Thy heavenly promises; Through Thy mercy, O our God, Who art blessed, and dost live, and govern all things, world without end. *Amen.*

The Twenty-First Sunday after Trinity.

O LORD Jesus Christ, to Whom Glory in the Highest is ever sung in Heaven and on earth; Grant unto us, and to all Thy people, Thy good will, cleanse us from all our sins, and give us Thy peace forever; Through Thy mercy, O our God, Who art blessed, and dost live, and govern all things, world without end. *Amen.*

The Twenty-second Sunday after Trinity.

O CHRIST our Lord, at Whose coming peace returned to earth, vouchsafe, we beseech Thee, to keep ever in Thy peace those whom Thou didst reconcile unto Thee by Thy first coming, until, at Thy coming again in glorious majesty, Thou makest them to inherit eternal peace; Through Thy mercy, O our God, Who art blessed, and dost live, and govern all things, world without end. *Amen.*

The Twenty-third Sunday after Trinity.

O LORD Jesus Christ; Be merciful unto us for Thy Name's sake, wherein we have wandered from Thee, bring us back, wash away the sins that we have committed, and set us, whom Thou hast redeemed, at Thy right hand, when Thou comest to be

our Judge; Through Thy mercy, O our God, Who
art blessed, and dost live, and govern all things, world
without end. *Amen.*

The Twenty-fourth Sunday after Trinity.

O LORD Jesus Christ, Who art the Redeemer of
all those who put their trust in Thee; Loose
Thy people, we pray thee, from the bonds of their
sins, fill their hearts and minds with true wisdom, and
let Thy peace and heavenly benediction ever be with
them; Through Thy mercy, O our God, Who art
blessed, and dost live and govern all things, world
without end. *Amen.*

*When there are Twenty-six Sundays between Trinity Sunday
and Advent Sunday, the Collect for the Sixth Sunday after the
Epiphany shall be used on the Twenty-fifth Sunday; and when
there are Twenty-seven such Sundays, the Collect for the Fifth
Sunday after the Epiphany shall be used on the Twenty-fifth
Sunday, and that for the Sixth Sunday after Epiphany, on the
Twenty-sixth Sunday.*

The Sunday next before Advent.

O LORD Jesus Christ, Son of the Living God,
Who healest the wounds of our sins, and Who
wilt shew goodness everlasting in the Land of the
Living; Grant that we may serve Thee faithfully with

a quiet mind in this world, and, going hence in Thy love, may praise and bless Thee forever in the world to come; Through Thy mercy, O our God, Who art blessed, and dost live, and govern all things, world without end. *Amen.*

Saint Andrew's Day.

ALMIGHTY God, Who didst give unto Thy blessed Apostle Saint Andrew such grace, that he readily heard the calling of Thy Son Jesus Christ, and followed Him without delay; Grant that we may, in like manner, follow Christ, despising the world which passeth away, and so attain to everlasting joys; Through the same. Jesus Christ our Lord. *Amen.*

Saint Thomas the Apostle.

O ALMIGHTY God, Who, that we might more surely believe, didst suffer Thine Holy Apostle Saint Thomas to doubt; Establish us, we pray Thee, in Thy true faith, and make us ever to serve Thee in such works as are agreeable to the same; Through Jesus Christ, Thy Son our Lord. *Amen.*

Saint Stephen's Day.

O LORD Jesus Christ, Who didst give unto Thy First Martyr, Saint Stephen, grace to follow Thine example both in suffering and in patience; Grant that, like him, in all our sufferings here for Thee, we may not be terrified by our adversaries, but may pray for those who would do us harm, to Thee, O Blessed Saviour, Who, with the Father and the Holy Ghost, livest and reignest, ever one God, world without end. *Amen.*

Saint John the Evangelist's Day.

O LORD Jesus Christ, Who didst have for Thine Apostle Saint John a special love; Grant us grace to love Thee as truly as he loved, and make us to share in the love that Thou hadst for Him; Through Thy mercy, O our God, Who art blessed, and dost live, and govern all things, world without end. *Amen.*

The Holy Innocents' Day.

O GOD, Who out of the mouths of babes and sucklings hast perfected praise, and madest infants to glorify Thee by the shedding of their blood; Mortify in us, we pray Thee, all evil desires, and give us a ready will to serve Thee with the simplicity of children and with the constancy of strong men; Through Jesus Christ our Lord. *Amen.*

The Conversion of Saint Paul.

O CHRIST, the Son of God, Who didst graciously choose Saint Paul to be Thine Apostle, and didst enable Him so to sow the good seed of Thy word throughout the world, that from it there has sprung up an abundant harvest unto Thee; Grant that his teachings may sink deep into our hearts, and bring forth fruit to Thy glory, Who, with the Father and the Holy Ghost, livest and reignest, ever one God, world without end. *Amen.*

The Presentation of Christ in the Temple,
Commonly called
The Purification of Saint Mary the Virgin.

A LMIGHTY and Everliving God, Who, as on this day, didst cause Thine Only-Begotten Son to be presented in the Temple in substance of our flesh; Grant that, with hearts and minds purified, we may be brought to behold Thine everlasting glory in Thy Temple on high; Through the same, Jesus Christ, our Lord. *Amen.*

Saint Matthias the Apostle.

O ALMIGHTY God, Who didst choose Thy faithful servant Matthias to take part in the Ministry and Apostleship from which Judas by transgression fell; Grant that Thy Church, preserved from false Apostles, may ever be blessed with faithful Ministers of Thy word and sacraments; Through Jesus Christ our Lord. *Amen.*

The Annunciation of the Blessed Virgin Mary.

O CHRIST, the Word of God Most High, Who wast made flesh that Thou mightest dwell amongst us; Pour Thy grace into our hearts and minds, that we, who have been redeemed by the Mystery of Thine Incarnation, may forever dwell with Thee; Through Thy mercy, O Christ our God, Who, with the Father and the Holy Ghost, livest and reignest, ever one God, world without end. *Amen.*

Saint Mark's Day.

O CHRIST,the Son of God, the Giver of all good gifts, Who hast watered all the ends of the earth with the fourfold stream of Thy Holy Gospels; Instruct us, we pray Thee, in the doctrine delivered

unto us by Thine Evangelist Saint Mark, and make
us to have a true fear and love of Thy Holy Name;
Through Thy mercy, O our God, Who art blessed,
and dost live, and govern all things, world without
end. *Amen.*

Saint Philip and Saint James, Apostles.

O LORD Jesus Christ, Who didst declare Thyself to Thine holy Apostles, Saint Philip and
Saint James, as the Way, the Truth, and the Life;
Grant, we pray Thee, that we may never depart from
the right way, but may so walk in Thy truth, that we
may attain to everlasting life in Thee; Through Thy
mercy, O Christ our God, Who, with the Father and
the Holy Ghost, art blessed, and dost live, and govern
all things, world without end. *Amen.*

Saint Barnabas the Apostle.

O FATHER of Mercies and God of all Consola-
tion; Fill us, we pray Thee, with Thy Holy
Spirit, so that, after the example of Thy blessed Apostle
Saint Barnabas, the Son of Consolation, we, loving
Thee above all things, may delight in doing good to
our fellow men; Through Jesus Christ our Lord.
Amen.

Saint John Baptist's Day.

O LORD Jesus Christ, Who didst make Thy Forerunner, Saint John Baptist, to be as a bright light in Thy Temple; Grant that we may ever shine in Thy Church, with the ardor of faith, in works of charity, and in true humility; Through Thy mercy, O Christ our God, Who, with the Father and the Holy Ghost, livest and reignest, ever one God, world without end. *Amen.*

Saint Peter's Day.

O CHRIST, the Son of the Living God, Whom Saint Peter, stablished on the true Rock, truly confessed; Grant us, we humbly beseech Thee, so to confess Thee, that, like him, we may obtain Thy blessing; Through Thy mercy, O Christ our God, Who, with the Father and the Holy Ghost, livest and reignest, ever one God, world without end. *Amen.*

Saint James the Apostle.

GRANT, O Lord, that as Thine holy Apostle Saint James, so soon as he was called, left the ship and his father, and followed Thy Son Jesus Christ with all his heart, so we may ever with a glad will obey Thy commandments; Through the same, Jesus Christ, our Lord. *Amen.*

Saint Bartholomew the Apostle.

O CHRIST, the Power of God, and the Wisdom of God, Who didst give to Thine holy Apostle Saint Bartholomew power to tread on serpents and scorpions; Strengthen us, we pray Thee, by Thy grace, that in Thy might we may vanquish and overcome all our spiritual enemies, and with pure hearts serve Thee, Whom, with the Father and the Holy Ghost, we worship and glorify, ever one God, world without end. *Amen.*

Saint Matthew the Apostle.

O LORD Jesus Christ, Who, of Thy great goodness, didst call Matthew the publican to be Thine Apostle and Evangelist; Grant us, like him, to withstand temptation, and, turning from all the allurements of the world, to follow Thee without delay; Through Thy mercy, O our God, Who art blessed, and dost live, and govern all things, world without end. *Amen.*

Saint Michael and All Angels.

O LORD, the King Eternal; Send, we pray Thee Thine Holy Angels to defend us both in soul and body; and grant that as Thou hast called us to share their blessedness in the world to come, so we may ever follow the example of their obedience, and delight to do Thy pleasure; Through Jesus Christ, Thy Son, our Lord. *Amen.*

Saint Luke the Evangelist.

O GOD, Who healest the infirmities of Thy people, and Who didst call Luke the beloved Physician to be an Evangelist and Physician of the soul; Grant that, in the wholesome doctrine of Thy word delivered through him, our souls may find an healing medicine; Through Jesus Christ, Thy Son, our Lord. *Amen.*

Saint Simon and Saint Jude, Apostles.

O ALMIGHTY God, Who hast built Thy Church upon the foundation of the Apostles and Prophets, Jesus Christ Himself being the Chief Corner Stone; Make us, we pray Thee, to be living stones in Thy Temple on High; Through the same, Jesus Christ, our Lord. *Amen.*

All Saints' Day.

O GOD, of Whose gift Thy blessed Saints, who are now at rest, overcame the world; Grant us now to follow in their footsteps, and after this life to be partakers with them of heavenly joys; Through Jesus Christ, Thy Son, our Lord. *Amen.*

The Ember-Days in Advent.

O LORD God, Who, at the first coming of Thy Son Jesus Christ, didst send John Baptist, in the spirit and power of Elias, to prepare the way before Him; Grant unto the ministers of Thy word and sacraments, with like burning zeal to prepare the way for His coming again; Through the same, Jesus Christ, our Lord. *Amen.*

The Ember-Days in Lent.

O LORD Jesus Christ, Who didst send Thine holy Apostles to preach among all nations repentance and remission of sins, through Thy name; Grant that through those now Thine ambassadors the erring may be brought to repentance, and the penitent stablished in Thy true faith; Through Thy mercy, O our God, Who art blessed, and dost live, and govern all things, world without end. *Amen.*

The Ember-Days in Whitsun-tide.

O GOD, Who, as at this time, didst send Thine Holy Ghost upon Thine Apostles, and didst so endue them with power from on high; Grant that the same Blessed Spirit, working in and through the ministers of Thy Church, may make the word preached and the sacraments administered by them effectual to the salvation of many souls; Through Thy mercy, and for the sake of Jesus Christ, Thy. Son, our Saviour. *Amen.*

The Ember-Days in Autumn.

O LORD of the Harvest; Grant, we humbly beseech Thee, that those whom Thou dost call to minister in Thy Holy Church, may ever abound in the work of the Lord, and that the fruit of their labors, approved of Thee, may endure unto everlasting life; Through Jesus Christ, Thy Son, our Lord. *Amen.*

Harvest Festival.

B LESSED Lord, Who hast crowned the year with Thy goodness, and made our fields to bring forth abundantly for the supply of our needs; We give Thee hearty thanks for all Thy benefits, beseeching Thee to give us grace ever to serve Thee, with a glad will, in this world, and, in the world to come, make us partakers of everlasting joys; Through Jesus Christ, our Lord, to Whom, with Thee and the Holy Ghost, be all honor and glory, world without end. *Amen.*

Additional Collects

Prayers.

For the Unity of the Church.

GRANT, O Lcrd, that Thy Church throughout the world may be held together in unity. Preserve it from heresies and schisms, and from all that might hinder godly concord. And as in heaven and on earth Thou art worshipped as one Lord, so may all mankind serve Thee in the unity of one faith; Through Jesus Christ, our Saviour, Who liveth and reigneth, with Thee and the Holy Ghost, ever one God, world without end. *Amen.*

For the Conversion of the Heathen.

MOST Gracious God, Who hast gathered into Thy Church a great company out of all nations; Fulfil, we pray Thee, what Thou hast foretold by Thy Holy Prophets, that all the ends of the world should remember themselves and be turned unto Thee; and make all the kindreds of the nations to worship before Thee; Through the only Saviour of the world, Thy Son, Jesus Christ, our Lord. *Amen.*

In Time of Affliction.

O LORD God, good and gracious; Grant that we may not be cast down under the afflictions Thou dost see fit to lay upon us, but may we, ever trusting in Thy goodness, be brought through the trials of this world to the joys of the life to come; Through Thy mercy, O our God, and for the sake of Jesus Christ, Thy Son, our Lord. *Amen.*

For Others in Affliction.

O GOD, Who despisest not the sighing of a contrite heart, nor the desire of such as are sorrowful; mercifully accept our prayers which we make for Thy servants now suffering adversity, and grant that those evils which either the devil or man worketh against them, may be brought to nought, and by Thy good Providence may be dispersed, that so, delivered from harm by Thy mercy, they may evermore give thanks unto Thee in Thy Holy Church; Through Jesus Christ, our Lord. *Amen.*

For Charity to the Poor.

MAKE us, O Lord, we beseech Thee, in obedience to Thy will, ever kind to the poor and needy, so that, abounding in works of mercy, we may be

inheritors of Thine eternal Kingdom; Through Thy
mercy, O our God, and for the sake of Him Who
gave Himself for us, Thy Son, Jesus Christ, our Lord.
Amen.

For Travelers.

DIRECT O Lord, in peace, we beseech Thee, the
way of Thy servants, *for whom we pray unto
Thee*, make *them*, if it be Thy will, to journey safely,
and fulfil *their* desires as may be most expedient for
them. Grant that what *they* now undertake in humble
dependence upon Thy goodness, *they* may complete
with hearts full of gratitude to Thee for Thine abundant
mercy; Through Jesus Christ, our Lord. *Amen.*

An Order

FOR DAILY FAMILY PRAYER,

FROM HOLY SCRIPTURE, AND THE MOZARABIC LITURGY.

Morning Prayer.

All standing up, let the Master of the house, or the person that represNeteth him, say:

I N the Name of Jesus Christ our Lord, light and peace be with us. *All*, Amen.

Or this:

I N the Name of the Father, and of the Son, and of the Holy Ghost. *All*, Amen.

Then shall be said the Proper Sentence and Response, according to what followeth:

In Advent.

The Lord cometh,
Ans. Who both will bring to light the hidden things of darkness, and will make manifest the counsels of the hearts. *1 Cor.*, iv: 5.

Christmas to Epiphany.

The dayspring from on high hath visited us,

Ans. To give light to them that sit in darkness.
St. Luke, i: 78, 79.

Epiphany to Septuagesima.

Jesus said, I am the Light of the world, he that
followeth Me shall not walk in darkness,

Ans. But shall have the light of life. *St. John*,
viii: 12.

Septuagesima to Lent.

Show the light of Thy countenance upon Thy
servant,

Ans. And teach me Thy statutes. *Ps.* cxix: 135.

Lent.

God be merciful unto us, and bless us,

Ans. And show us the light of His countenance,
and be merciful unto us. *Ps.* lxvii: 1.

Easter to Ascension.

Christ hath abolished death,

Ans. And brought life and immortality to light,
through the Gospel. *2 Tim.*, i: 10.

Ascension to Whitsun-day.

O send out Thy light and Thy truth,

 Ans. That they may lead me, and bring me unto Thy holy hill, and to Thy dwelling. *Ps.* xliii: 3.

Whitsun-day to Trinity Sunday.

With Thee is the well of life,

 Ans. And in Thy light shall we see light. *Psalm* xxxvi: 9.

Trinity to Advent.

God is Light, and in Him is no darkness at all.　If we walk in the light, as He is in the light, we have fellowship one with another,

 Ans. And the Blood of Jesus Christ, His Son, cleanseth us from all sin. *1 John*, i: 5, 7.

Saints' Days.

Light is sown for the righteous,

 Ans. And gladness for the upright in heart. *Ps.* xcvii: 11.

Then may be said one of Penitential Psalms, with accompanying Prayers (pp. 61–64).

Then shall be said or sung, by all together:

Glory and honor be to the Father, and to the Son, and to the Holy Ghost, world without end. Amen.

(Whenever this Gloria occurs in this Order, it is to be sung, or said, by all together :

Or, instead thereof, may be sung, or said, as followeth :

Glory be to the Father, and to the Son, and to the Holy Ghost ;

Ans. As it was in the beginning, is now, and ever shall be, world without end. Amen.)

From the rising up of the sun, unto the going down of the same,

Ans. The Lord's Name be praised.

Blessed be the Name of the Lord, from this time forth, for evermore.

Ans. The Lord's Name be praised.

Then may be sung, or said, a Psalm, or part of a Psalm, followed by a Gloria.

Then may be read a Lesson from the Old, or the New Testament.

And before a Lesson from the Old Testament, shall be said :

The Blessing of God Almighty, Who spake in time past unto the fathers by the Prophets, be upon you that hear His Holy Word,

Ans. And upon you that read it.

And before a Lesson from the New Testament, shall be said :

The Blessing of God Almighty, Who hath, in these last days, spoken unto us by His Son, be upon you that hear His Holy Word,

Ans.　And upon you that read it.

After such Lesson, may be sung, or said, Benedictus es (p. 65), Benedictus (p. 66), one of the Glorias, or a suitable Hymn.

Then shall be said, all standing, the Apostles' Creed :

I BELIEVE in God the Father Almighty, Maker of heaven and earth :

And in Jesus Christ His only Son our Lord; Who was conceived by the Holy Ghost, Born of the Virgin Mary; Suffered under Pontius Pilate, Was crucified, dead, and buried; He descended into hell, The third day He rose from the dead; He ascended into heaven, And sitteth on the right hand of God the Father Almighty; From thence He shall come to judge the quick and the dead.

I believe in the Holy Ghost; The holy Catholic Church; The Communion of Saints; The Forgiveness of sins; The Resurrection of the body; And the Life everlasting. Amen.

Then shall be said :

The Lord be ever with you.

Ans. And with thy Spirit.

Let us pray.

Then shall be said the following prayers, all devoutly kneeling:

Lord have mercy upon us.

Ans. Christ have mercy upon us.

Lord have mercy upon us.

Then shall be said, by all together, the Lord's Prayer.

OUR Father, Who art in Heaven, Hallowed be Thy Name. Thy Kingdom come. Thy will be done on earth, As it is in Heaven. Give us this day our daily bread. And forgive us our trespasses, As we forgive those who trespass against us. And lead us not into temptation; But deliver us from evil. Amen.

Deliver us from evil, and confirm us in Thy fear, O Triune God, and make us, with unceasing service, to serve Thee, our God and our Lord, Who livest, and governest all things, world without end. *Amen.*

O Lord, show Thy mercy upon us.

Ans. And grant us Thy salvation.

O Lord, save our country.

Ans. And mercifully hear us when we call upon Thee.

Endue Thy ministers with righteousness.

Ans. And make Thy chosen people joyful.

O Lord, save Thy people.

Ans. And bless Thine inheritance.

Give peace in our time, O Lord.

Ans. For it is Thou, Lord, only, that makest us dwell in safety.

O God, make clean our hearts within us.

Ans. And take not Thy Holy Spirit from us.

Then shall be said the Collect for the Day, after which may be said the Collect for the Season.

Then shall be said the Collects following:

A Collect for Peace.

O GOD, the Author of peace; Shed abroad, we pray Thee, Thy peace in our hearts and minds; guard and protect us in all dangers, and make us, ever trusting in Thy defence, to serve Thee without fear, all the days of our life; Through Jesus Christ our Lord. *Amen.*

A Collect for Grace.

O LORD Jesus Christ, Who didst take upon Thee the weakness of our mortal nature; Grant that we may pass this day in safety, and without sin, resisting all the temptations of the enemy, and that at eventide we may joyfully praise Thee, O King Eternal; Through Thy mercy, O our God, Who art blessed, and dost live, and govern all things, world without end. *Amen.*

Then may be said any selected Collects or Prayers, after which shall be said as followeth :

MAY the Everlasting God bless us this day; may He save and defend us from all that is evil, and make us, at last, partakers of His heavenly kingdom; Through Jesus Christ our Lord. *Amen.*

Then may be said, all standing up:

IN the Name of Jesus Christ our Lord, may we go to the work to which we are called this day, in peace. *All.* Amen.

Evening Prayer.

The order for Daily Family Prayer, in the Evening, is the same as that for the Morning, except that the Canticles, to be sung or said after a Lesson, are Magnificat (p. 67) or Nunc Dimittis (p. 68) ; and except, also, that the Collects, etc., to be said after the Collect for the Day (and that for the Season, if it be said), are as followeth :

A Collect for Peace.

O GOD, from Whom all good things do come ; Strengthen Thy people, we pray thee, against all adversities, and fill them with Thy peace, so that with a quiet mind they may give glory to Thee in Thy Holy Temple, and, forgetting all earthly ills, may ever render Thee honor and praise ; Through Jesus Christ our Lord. *Amen.*

A Collect for Aid against Perils.

O LORD, Who hast preserved us during the labors of the day ; Guard us, we pray Thee, through the dangers of the night, let Thine Holy Spirit watch over us, and be now, and evermore, our defence ; Through Jesus Christ, Thy Son, our Lord. *Amen.*

Then may be said any selected Collects or Prayers, after which shall be said as followeth:

MAY the Lord hear us and bless us; may He save us from our spiritual enemy, and from all that is evil, and keep us under the shadow of His wings, this night and for evermore; Through Jesus Christ our Lord. *Amen.*

Then may be said, all standing up:

IN the Name of Jesus Christ our Lord, may we have quiet sleep this night, and rest in peace. *All,* Amen.

PENITENTIAL PSALMS,

With accompanying Prayers and Versicles.

I.

The Lord be ever with you.

Ans. And with thy spirit.

Then, all kneeling, shall be said, by alternate verses, or by all together, from the Fifty-first Psalm, as followeth:

Miserere mei, Deus.

HAVE mercy upon me, O God, after Thy great goodness: according to the multitude of Thy mercies do away mine offences.

Wash me throughly from my wickedness: and cleanse me from my sin.

For I acknowledge my faults: and my sin is ever before me.

Against Thee only have I sinned, and done this evil in Thy sight: that Thou mightest be justified in Thy saying, and clear when Thou art judged.

Behold, I was shapen in wickedness: and in sin hath my mother conceived me.

But lo, Thou requirest truth in the inward parts: and shalt make me to understand wisdom secretly.

Turn Thy face from my sins: and put out all my misdeeds.

Make me a clean heart, O God: and renew a right spirit within me.

Cast me not away from Thy presence: and take not Thy holy Spirit from me.

Glory and honor be to the Father, and to the Son, and to the Holy Ghost, world without end. Amen.

Then shall be said:

TURN Thy face from our sins, O Lord, and put out all our misdeeds; Look not upon our evil doings, but lend a merciful ear to our confessions; And since Thou art pleased with the sacrifice of a broken and a contrite heart, grant that we may offer this which Thou dost require, and may so obtain the pardon which Thou dost promise the penitent; Through Jesus Christ our Lord. Amen.

Then shall be said :

OUR Father, Who art in Heaven, Hallowed be Thy name. Thy kingdom come. Thy will be done on earth, As it is in Heaven. Give us this day our daily bread. And forgive us our trespasses, As we forgive those who trespass against us. And lead us not into temptation; But deliver us from evil. Amen.

O Lord, open Thou our lips.

Ans. And our mouth shall show forth Thy praise.

O God, make speed to save us.

Ans. O Lord, make haste to help us.

II.

The Lord be ever with you.

Ans. And with thy spirit.

Then, all kneeling, shall be said, by alternate verses, or by all together, the One Hundred and Thirtieth Psalm, as followeth :

De profundis.

OUT of the deep have I called unto Thee, O Lord : Lord, hear my voice.

O let Thine ears consider well : the voice of my complaint.

If Thou, Lord, wilt be extreme to mark what is done amiss : O Lord, who may abide it ?

For there is mercy with Thee : therefore shalt Thou be feared.

I look for the Lord; my soul doth wait for Him : in His word is my trust.

My soul fleeth unto the Lord : before the morning watch; I say, before the morning watch.

O Israel, trust in the Lord; for with the Lord there is mercy : and with Him is plenteous redemption.

And He shall redeem Israel : from all his sins.

Glory and honor be to the Father, and to the Son, and to the Holy Ghost, world without end.   Amen.

Then shall be said :

HEAR our prayer, O Lord, incline Thine ear unto our calling; We acknowledge our faults, we would not hide from Thee our sins; Against Thee, only, have we sinned, and confessing we entreat Thy favor; We have erred from Thy commandments, and have not kept Thy law; Turn Thee, O Lord, and deliver Thy servants, pardon our sins, and, of Thy great goodness, bestow on us Thine abundant mercy, for the sake of Him who shed His Precious Blood to redeem us, Thy Son, Jesus Christ, our Lord. Amen.

Then shall be said:

OUR Father, Who art in Heaven.........
.........But deliver us from evil. Amen.
O Lord, open Thou our lips.
Ans. And our mouth shall shew forth Thy praise.
O God, make speed to save us.
Ans. O Lord, make haste to help us.

CANTICLES.

The following Canticles are to be sung, or said, one of the first two after a Lesson at Morning Prayer, one of the last two after a Lesson at Evening Prayer.

After each Canticle, is to be sung, or said: Glory and honor, etc., *or* Glory be to the Father, etc.

Benedictus es.

BLESSED art Thou, O Lord God of our fathers: and to be praised and exalted above all forever.
And blessed is Thy glorious and holy Name: and to be praised and exalted above all forever.

Blessed art Thou in the temple of Thine holy glory: and to be praised and glorified above all forever.

Blessed art Thou that beholdest the depths, and sittest upon the cherubim: and to be praised and exalted above all forever.

Blessed art Thou on the glorious Throne of Thy kingdom: and to be praised and glorified above all forever.

Blessed art Thou in the firmament of heaven: and to be praised and glorified above all forever.

Benedictus. St. Luke, i: 68.

BLESSED be the Lord God of Israel: for He hath visited, and redeemed His people;

And hath raised up a mighty salvation for us: in the house of His servant David;

As He spake by the mouth of His holy Prophets: which have been since the world began;

That we should be saved from our enemies: and from the hands of all that hate us;

To perform the mercy promised to our forefathers: and to remember His holy Covenant;

To perform the oath which He sware to our forefather Abraham: that He would give us;

That we being delivered out of the hands of our enemies: might serve Him without fear;

In holiness and righteousness before Him: all the days of our life.

And thou, Child, shalt be called the Prophet of the Highest: for thou shalt go before the face of the Lord to prepare His ways;

To give knowledge of salvation unto His people: for the remission of their sins,

Through the tender mercy of our God: whereby the day-spring from on high hath visited us;

To give light to them that sit in darkness, and in the shadow of death: and to guide our feet into the way of peace.

Magnificat. St. Luke, i: 46.

MY soul doth magnify the Lord; and my spirit hath rejoiced in God my Saviour.

For He hath regarded: the lowliness of His handmaiden.

For behold, from henceforth: all generations shall call me blessed.

For He that is mighty hath magnified me: And holy is His Name.

And His mercy is on them that fear Him: throughout all generations.

He hath shewed strength with His arm: He hath scattered the proud in the imagination of their hearts.

He hath put down the mighty from their seat: and hath exalted the humble and meek.

He hath filled the hungry with good things: and the rich He hath sent empty away.

He remembering His mercy hath holpen His servant Israel: as He promised to our forefathers, Abraham and his seed, forever.

Nunc dimittis. St. Luke, ii: 29.

LORD, now lettest Thou Thy servant depart in peace: according to Thy word.

For mine eyes have seen: Thy salvation.

Which Thou hast prepared: before the face of all people.

To be a light to lighten the Gentiles: and to be the glory of Thy people, Israel.

Appendix.

I. THE AIM OF THIS BOOK.

THE learned Canon Bright, in his ANCIENT COL-
LECTS, of which, whether it be considered as a
most useful book of devotion, or as a work of liturgical scholarship, one could hardly speak too highly,
gives a number of prayers translated from what he
well describes as "the glowing and pathetic supplica-
tions of the Ancient Spanish Church."

It has been thought that a fuller selection of such
prayers from the Mozarabic Liturgy, giving the Collects for the Sundays and other chief Holy Days of
the Christian Year, with some additional prayers,
might aid the devotions of persons to whom hallowed words, instinct with the same spirit which
breathes in the Collects of our Prayer Book, and,
like those Collects, a legacy from the earlier days of
the Church, are ever acceptable.

Care has been taken, in translating, to keep as
close as might be to the original, except that, not
infrequently, what seemed over-long expressions
have been condensed, the prayers of the Ancient
Spanish Church being scarcely more marked by fer-

vency, than by exuberance of diction. As an instance, it may be mentioned that in the Mozarabic Liturgy there are more than one hundred different Proper Prefaces, of which quite a number are longer than the Exhortation in our Communion Office, " Dearly Beloved in the Lord, etc.," and some of them twice its length. The originals of several Collects are given in the following pages, and at another time the original Latin of all may be published.

2. THE MOZARABIC LITURGY.[*]

BY the term " The Mozarabic Liturgy" is designated the liturgy in general use in the Spanish Church from the time of St. Isidore of Seville, who,

---

[*] Those wishing further information in regard to the Mozarabic Liturgy are referred to

Essays on Liturgiology ; By the Rev. J. M. Neale, D. D.

Introduction to the History of the Holy Eastern Church ; By the same.

Liturgies Eastern and Western ; By the Rev. C. E. Hammond.

The Mozarabic Liturgy for the First Sunday in Advent : By the Rev. Samuel Hart.

The Mozarabic Liturgy, a paper, by the Rev. Augustus Jackson, in the *Church Eclectic*, Nov. 1880.

The Mozarabic Liturgy and Mexican Church Reform, a paper, by the present writer, in the *American Church Review*, April, 1876.

about the beginning of the seventh century, had much to do with putting it into its present form, until the eleventh century, when it was almost entirely set aside, through Romish influence. In its essential features, it would seem to have been coeval with the implanting of Christianity in Spain, and, continued in use, in a very few Spanish churches, even to this day, it has providentially remained a living rite. As to the name *Mozarabic*, Neale says : " The real derivation is simple enough : *Arab Arabe* signifying an Arab by descent (like an Hebrew of the Hebrews), *Arab Most-Arabe* an Arab by adoption, and the latter term having been gradually softened and applied to the Liturgy."*

3. COLLECTS FOR THE SEASONS.

THE Book of Common Prayer, directing the Collects for the First Sunday in Advent, and for Ash Wednesday, to be repeated each day during the seasons at the head of which those days respectively stand, makes of them Collects for the Season. The Mozarabic Liturgy provides Collects for that specific purpose. The Collect for Easter-tide, in the original, is as follows :

---

* Essays on Liturgiology, p. 131.

TE excelsa laus in altissimis decet, Tibi e terris gloriam Ecclesia canit, atque hujus catervae concentus ad astra hymnum emittit : Rogamus Te, Omnipotens Deus, ut sicut Tuas solenniter porrigimus laudes, ita precum nostrarum jubeas efficaciter suscipere voces. *Amen.*

Per misericordiam Tuam, Deus noster, Qui es benedictus, et vivis, et omnia regis, in saecula saeculorum. *Amen.**

This double ending is very common with Mozarabic Collects. In the translation it has been retained only in the case of Collects for the Seasons.

4. COLLECTS FOR THE SUNDAYS AND HOLY DAYS.

FOR the most part, the Collects for the Sundays, and for the Festivals of our Lord, have been translated from the Latin originals without other change than needful condensation. It has not always been possible, however, to take them from the service of a corresponding day. For the most of the Sundays after Trinity there were no special services appointed. When a Saint's Day service was not said on such day, as was generally the case, the service of a preceding Sunday was repeated.

---

* Liturgia Mozarabica, I. 479.

The Collect for the Third Sunday after the Epiphany, in the original Latin, is as follows:

A DESTO, Deus Pater Omnipotens, precibus nostris, et plenitudinem nobis tribue charitatis et pacis; ut omnes nos qui de misericordiâ Tuâ confidimus, in spe semper, et charitate, sine fine vivamus. *Amen.**

The Collect in our Prayer Book for the Sunday after the Ascension, is taken, as is well known, from the Vesper Antiphon of the Ascension, with whose words the Venerable Bede breathed forth his soul at Yarrow. Canon Bright† and Dean Goulburn‡ express the regret which others feel, that our Reformers did not continue "its ancient character as an appeal to the Son, the ascended King of Glory." The original of the Collect for Ascension Day in this book, a *Capitula* at Lauds on that Festival, is as follows:

D OMINE Rex Gloriæ, Qui patefactis et adimpletis Prophetarum oraculis, tamquam elevatis æternalibus portis, Paternam repetis sedem, quia dum tua Deitas eo quo nunquam discessit regreditur,

---

*Liturgia Mozarabica, Edit. Migne. I. 255.

†Ancient Collects, p. 202, 3d edit., 1864. ‡The Collects of the Day, Vol I, 403, 404.

humano generi coelorum aditus aperitur; Dona ut
illic extendatur nostra intentio, quo praecessit vera
nostra Redemptio, nec inhaereamus captivâ dilec-
tatione terrenis, cum jam nostri corporis Caput Tecum
regnat in coelis.*

When we come to the Collects for the Saints' Days,
greater changes have in some cases been required.
And yet it has been possible to find fitting material
for such Collects in the Mozarabic Liturgy, to a much
larger extent than the framers of our Prayer Book
could in the Use of Sarum. In the Prayer Book, the
Collect for Holy Innocents' Day is, in the main,
Gelasian; those for the Purification, the Annunciation, St. John Baptist's Day, and St. Michael's are
Gregorian; those for St. Stephen's Day, the Conversion of St. Paul, and St. Bartholomew's Day are, in
part, from ancient sources; the rest date from 1549,
1552, and 1661. In this book, while the Collects
for the Festivals of St. Matthias and St. Barnabas
have something from the Mozarabic, all the other
Saints' Day Collects have originals to which they
correspond, in no inadequate degree, in the Ancient
Spanish Liturgy. What follows, the original of the
Collect for St. Peter's Day, shows what good mate-

*Liturgia Mozarabica, II. 657.

rial we have offered us, and, at the same time, what changes must needs be made in using it.

CHRISTE, Filius Dei Vivi, Quem Petrus super petram solidatus verè confessus est, quia utique non petra a Petro, sed Petrus vocatus est a petrâ in quâ est fundata Ecclesia; Te supplices deprecamur, ut idem qui accepit claves regni coelorum peccatoribus pandat coelestis viae introitum, ut per quem doctrinae sublimis exempla suscepimus, per eum aeternae vitae nos suscepisse commoda sentiamus. *Amen.*

Per misericordiam, etc.*

5. ADDITIONAL COLLECTS AND PRAYERS.

UNDER this heading but a few examples have been given. It would be easy, should this be called for, to largely increase the number.

The original of the " Prayer for those in Affliction " resembles, while differing from it in several particulars, the original of a prayer in our Litany.† The Mozarabic form is as follows:

DEUM, Qui contritorum non despicit gemitum, et moerentium non aspernatur affectum, lachrymosis precibus fratres dilectissimi supplicemus, ut

---

* Liturgia Mozarabica, II. 1105.
†This, a Collect "*pro tribulatione cordis*" in the Use of Sarum, may be found in Palmer's *Origines Liturgicae*, Vol. I, p. 299; and in Blunt's *Annotated Prayer Book*, p. 59.

hanc singularis victimae hostiam quam pro tribulatis
servis suis N., ad relevationem fidenter offerimus,
dignetur acceptare propitius, tribuatque ut quicquid
contra eos diabolica atque humana molivit adversitas
ad nihilum redigat, et consilio pietatis allidat, ut in
nullo de adversis laesi, Eidem mereantur illaesi offerre
sacrificium.*

6. AN ORDER FOR FAMILY PRAYER.

A T the suggestion of a Right Reverend friend,
"An Order for Family Prayer" has been arranged, from the Mozarabic Liturgy and Holy Scrip-
ture. To adapt it to varying circumstances and
needs, provision has been made for shortening or
lengthening the Order, as may be desired.

The originals of a Mozarabic Invocation and
Gloria, differing from those in use amongst us, are
as follows:

I N Nomine Domini Nostri Jesu Christi, lumen
cum pace.†

G LORIA et honor Patri, et Filio, et Spiritui
Sancto, in saecula saeculorum. Amen.‡

---

*Liturgia Mozarabica, I, 999.
†Liturgia Mozarabica, II. 47. ‡ Ibid, I. 109.

The first of the Canticles given, *Benedictus es*, consists of the introductory words of the Song of the Three Children. The others are, as will be seen, the three Evangelical Hymns.

7. WHAT IS PRAYED FOR IN THE COLLECTS OF THIS BOOK.

THE following classification of these Collects, according to their subjects, may be helpful to persons desiring to make use of them:

Preparation for Christ's Coming. Advent to Christmas, Ascension to Whitsun-day, First and Second in Advent, Sunday after Christmas, Twenty-third after Trinity.

The Benefits of Christ's Sacrifice. Palm Sunday (2d Coll.), Good Friday (1st Coll.).

Forgiveness. Ash Wednesday, Eleventh after Trinity.

Cleansing from Sin. Fifth after Epiphany, Septuagesima, Easter Even, Easter Day, Sunday after Ascension, Second, Third, Twenty-first and Twenty-third after Trinity, Purification.

Deliverance from Sin as a Disease. St. Luke.

Deliverance from the Bonds of Sin. Christmas to Septuagesima, Tenth and Twenty-fourth after Trinity.

Spiritual Sustenance.   First and Second in Lent,
Twelfth after Trinity.

Help in Spiritual Danger.   Fourth in Advent, First
in Lent, Fifteenth after Trinity, St. Bartholomew, St.
Matthew.

Support in Danger and Trouble.   Collects for Grace
and for Aid against Perils, Benedictions in the Order
for Family Prayer, Collect in time of Affliction, Prayer
for those in Affliction.   (A. C. & P., p. 50).

Angelic Help.   St. Michael.

Protection on a Journey.   (A. C. & P., p. 51).

Temporal Blessings.   Circumcision (2d Coll.), Rogation Days, Ninth after Trinity; *Thanksgiving for* ——,
Harvest Festival.

Spiritual Wisdom.   Whitsun-day to Trinity Sunday,
Epiphany, Fourth in Lent, First and Second after
Easter, Rogation Days, Whitsun-day, Fifth, Twelfth,
Nineteenth and Twenty-fourth after Trinity, St. Mark·

Grace to serve God Gladly.   Circumcision, Sixth
and Fourteenth after Trinity, St. Andrew, Holy Innocents, St. James, St. Michael.

Grace to serve God Faithfully.   Circumcision (2d
Coll.), Fifth in Lent, Second after Easter, Rogation
Days, Trinity Sunday, Thirteenth, Eighteenth, Nine-

teenth and Twentieth after Trinity, Sunday before Advent, St. Thomas, St. John Baptist, All Saints, "Deliver us from evil, etc." (Ord. Fam. Pr.).

True Repentance. Third in Advent.

Faith. Fourth after Easter, Trinity Sunday, St. Thomas.

Hope. Fourth in Lent.

Charity. Third after Epiphany, St. John the Evangelist.

Faith, Hope and Charity. Fourteenth after Trinity.

Joy. Easter to Ascension, Palm Sunday (1st Coll.).

Peace. First, Seventh, Twenty-first, Twenty-second and Twenty-fourth after Trinity, Collects for Peace (Ord. Fam. Pr.).

Peacefulness. Sixth after Epiphany, Seventeenth after Trinity.

True Love of Friends. Sexagesima, St. Barnabas.

Love of Enemies. Sexagesima, St. Stephen.

Charity to the Poor. (A. C. & P., p. 50).

The Welfare of the Church. Good Friday (2d Coll.), (A. C. & P., p. 49).

The Clergy. The Ember Day Collects.

The Conversion of the Heathen. (A. C. & P., p. 49).
That we may ever remain God's faithful children.
Christmas.

The Spirit of Adoption. Eighth after Trinity.

Heavenly-mindedness. Lent, Ascension to Whitsunday, Saints' Days, First and Fourth after Epiphany, Ascension Day, Fourth and Twentieth after Trinity, St. Andrew.

Everlasting Blessedness. Lent, First in Advent, Circumcision, Second, Fourth and Fifth after Epiphany, Septuagesima, Easter Even, Easter Day, First and Fifth after Easter, Sunday after Ascension, First, Fourth, Thirteenth, Sixteenth, Twentieth, Twenty-second and Twenty-third after Trinity, Sunday before Advent, St. Andrew, Purification, Annunciation, St. Philip and St. James, All Saints.

THE END.

www.ingramcontent.com/pod-product-compliance
Lightning Source LLC
Chambersburg PA
CBHW021427090426
42742CB00009B/1294